EMERGING FROM THE CHRYSALIS
REVERIES OF THE TRANSGENDER
by Jimi Bush

Introducing -
"Emerging From the Chrysalis:
Reveries of the Transgender Woman"

In this poignant and surreal collection
of poetry, Emerging From the
Chrysalis - Reveries of the
Transgender Woman explores the
profound journey of transformation,
identity, and self-discovery. These
poems traverse the emotional
landscapes of hope, despair, resilience,
and love as they illuminate the
multifaceted experiences of
transgender women.

From gardens blooming with hidden
truths to mirrors reflecting fragmented
souls, each piece paints an evocative
portrait of a woman reclaiming her light.
The verses weave through the
struggles of societal rejection, the inner
battles of duality, and the tender
moments of being seen and cherished.

This collection captures the raw
beauty of becoming in all its forms: the
quiet breaking of chains, the
shattering of masks, and the delicate
2

yet unyielding emergence into authenticity. Emerging From the Chrysalis is a celebration of perseverance and the boundless courage it takes to transform one's life and soul.

With surreal imagery and heartfelt introspection, this book invites readers to step into the shoes of those who defy convention to become the truest version of themselves—a journey of liberation, love, and light. For anyone seeking to understand or feel understood, this collection will stay with you long after the final page.

A luminous tribute to the transgender experience, told with grace, power, and unapologetic truth.

Welcome to the universe of...
The CelestialPainter.

I hope you enjoy,
Jimi/Jennifer Grayce

"A Challenging Path"

Her name is whispered
in the winds of time,
A riddle wrapped
in rhythm and rhyme.
On a chessboard sky,
where stars align,
She moves her pieces,
one bold design.

The pawns are fears,
small yet near,
Each step forward
weighted with fear.
The knights are dreams,
leaping high,
Across the black-and-white
divide of the sky.

Her queen, her truth,
moves far and wide,
Guarded fiercely,

her soul's raw pride.
The rooks are walls
she's scaled before,
Brick by brick,
from core to shore.

Life whispers,
"Make your move,
Each choice you make
will shape your groove."
Her hands tremble,
yet she stays,
Navigating
this complex maze.

The board stretches,
surreal and vast,
Every move
a ghost of her past.
The bishops glide
like doubts in disguise,
Slanting shadows,
distorting lies.

She falters, pauses,
heart in hand,
The future shifting
like desert sand.
"Can I make it?
Can I play this game,
And still hold on
to my own name?"

The clock ticks loud,
the hour is late,
But she knows her courage
will seal her fate.
Her fingers lift,
a piece takes flight,
She claims her space
in the endless fight.

Through traps and trials,
her spirit burns,
A guiding flame
where the path twists and turns.
Each victory small,

yet profound,
Each loss a lesson,
a wisdom found.

At the board's end
stands a glowing door,
A light she's dreamed of
forevermore.
Beyond it,
freedom sings her name,
A symphony born
from struggle and flame.

"This path is hard,
this path is mine,
Each move a step
to the divine.
The reward ahead
is worth the pain,
For in this game,
my truth shall reign."

With one last move,
she claims the throne,
The board dissolves,
she's not alone.
Her challenging path
has forged her soul,
A queen at last,
radiant and whole.

"A Complicated Sadness"

Beneath a sky
that shivers blue,
She stands where sunlight
filters through.
Joy blooms like roses
in her chest,
But sadness lingers,
an uninvited guest.

Her laughter spills
in golden streams,
Dancing with echoes
of fractured dreams.
Her steps are light,
her heart takes flight,
Yet shadows follow,
soft and tight.

"Why do I cry
when the world feels warm?
Why does this peace
still birth a storm?"
Her questions rise like smoke,
unseen,

Curling through
the spaces between.

Her joy is a symphony,
wild and bright,
A kaleidoscope spinning
in endless light.
Her sadness, a whisper,
soft and low,
A lullaby sung
by the ghosts she knows.

In her veins,
rivers of longing flow,
Twisting through valleys
of highs and lows.
Her body, a temple,
rebuilt with care,
Yet the past still lingers,
heavy and bare.

She watches
the moon's silvery guise,
Its face serene,
yet weeping skies.
"Is this my reflection?"

she wonders aloud,
"Both radiant
and wrapped in cloud?"

The world answers
in surreal hues,
With laughter in greens,
and sorrow in blues.
She gathers the colors,
paints her name,
A masterpiece wrought
from joy and shame.

"A complicated sadness,"
she muses with grace,
"Is the truth I wear,
the map of my face.
It sharpens my joy,
it deepens my pain,
A tapestry woven
in sun and rain."

And so she walks,
a paradox alive,
Through fields where
wild emotions thrive.
For in her heart,
a fire burns,
Of lessons lived
and paths she's earned.

Her sadness smiles,
her joy takes flight,
A dance of opposites
in the night.
"I am both, and I am whole,"
she sings,
A complicated sadness,
with radiant wings.

"A Heart Torn Between Two Faces"

In the garden
where mirrors bloom,
She walks among
the fractured moon.
Each shard a face,
a whispered plea,
Reflections of what
she'll never be.

A thousand eyes gaze
from the mist,
Each one a life
she's never kissed.
Lips like rivers,
flowing in pain,
Kissing shadows
that leave no stain.

Her heart, a clock
with broken hands,
Ticks through time's

unspoken sands.
One face smiles,
the other weeps,
Between them,
a love she never keeps.

The sky is stitched
with threads of red,
Wounds of stars
where dreams have bled.
She reaches up,
her fingers fray,
Touching truths
that melt away.

In her chest,
a hollow tune,
A song that ends
too soon, too soon.
Each note a tear,
each chord a sigh,
For faces lost
beneath the sky.

And yet she dances,
shattered whole,
A broken prism,
a radiant soul.
Through tears,
she finds her fleeting grace,
A heart torn
between every face.

"A Kaleidoscope of Shifting Lies"

She walks through
the tapestry of days,
a mosaic woven
from a billion stares,
each gaze a needle s
titching her shadow,
each blink,
a ripple across her name.

To one, she is a bird
of molten gold,
soaring through
the blistering sun,
her wings scattering
fragments of time—
moments
too sharp to hold.

To another,
she is a whispered ghost,
a flicker

in the fog of memory,
a candle lit
in an abandoned cathedral,
its wax melting
into ancient prayers.

In the eyes of a child,
she is a comet,
braiding the sky
with impossible hues,
a promise scrawled
in cosmic ink—
that wonder is
forever.

The lovers see her
as a tempest,
her heart an orchestra
of unruly storms,
thunder kissing
the edges of their longing,
lightning igniting
their quiet despair.

Yet the cynics paint her
as a riddle,
a kaleidoscope
of shifting lies,
her truth
a deck of shuffled cards,
the Joker
always smiling on top.

And she wonders,
who am I beneath this gaze?
A million selves
unravel and reweave,
their threads tangling
into unseen shapes,
her essence a melody
no one can sing.

For the world
does not see her;
it reflects
itself—
its fears,

its dreams,
its cracked
and radiant truths.

But she is none
of these things,
and
all of them,
a solitary flame
dancing between
a billion mirrors.

"A Time of Rebirth"

She stood at the edge
of a nameless dream,
Bound by chains
of a silent scream.
The world had carved
her a brittle mold,
A cage of iron,
a story untold.

In mirrors,
shadows wore her face,
A fractured mask,
a stolen space.
Their voices weighed
like granite skies,
"You must conform,"
their endless cries.

But deep within,
a fire burned,
A star unspoken,

a soul unturned.
Her veins pulsed songs
of ancient light,
A symphony yearning
to rewrite.

She tore the chains
with trembling hands,
Each link dissolving
like grains of sand.
The weight of "should"
fell to the ground,
And silence screamed
a freeing sound.

Her skin turned liquid,
her form anew,
A dance of colors
no one knew.
The sky wept pearls;
the earth took flight,
As she transformed
beneath the night.

From broken stone,
she rose in bloom,
A flower defying
its earthly tomb.
Her body, her temple,
no longer theirs,
Her truth a beacon,
climbing stairs.

"This is my time,"
she softly said,
"To live, to thrive,
to forge ahead."
No more shadows,
no more disguise,
She wore the stars
as her only ties.

The world still watched
with doubting eyes,
But she stood unbroken,
reaching the skies.
For in her heart,
she had given birth
To a timeless moment—
a time of rebirth.

"A Time Where Scars Run Deep"

Jennifer walks
through the clockwork maze,
Each tick a tremor,
each tock a blaze.
Shadows whisper
with voices torn,
Of bones betrayed
and hearts reborn.

Voice of Doubt:
"You'll never be real,
just fractured stone."
"A truthless echo,
forever alone."

Her hands clutch air,
yet hold her ground,
Her breath a hymn,
her heart unbound.

In the mirrors of time,
her face divides,
One of courage,
one that hides.

Voice of Fear:
"Feel the weight
of their biting stare."
"You're not enough—
you're barely there."

But deep within,
a spark ignites,
A rainbow flickers
in velvet nights.
Through storm-wracked skies,
it arcs and bends,
A spectral promise,
a light that mends.

Voice of Truth:
" Jennifer,
rise from the broken past."
"Your light is yours,
forever vast."

The clock strikes twelve;
the shadows wail,
But Jennifer's steps
begin to sail.
Her scars, like stars,
begin to shine,
Each one a fragment
of the divine.

Voice of Hope:
"You are the rainbow
that darkness fears."
"You are the keeper
of infinite years."

Through ticking worlds
and whispered scorn,
Jennifer walks,
her spirit reborn.
She threads her soul
through the night's embrace,
A time where scars
weave endless grace.

Let the clock tick on,
let shadows creep,
Jennifer stands
where scars run deep.
Her light transcends
their fleeting spite,
She is the dawn
after endless night.

"Another Broken Day"

The morning cracks
like porcelain skies,
Each shard a fragment
of whispered lies.
The sun limps forward,
its light askew,
Spilling over
a world she barely knew.

Her mirror holds a face
not quite her own,
A collage of battles
she's fought alone.
Her eyes are rivers,
flowing upstream,
Her lips a lock
on an unspoken dream.

"You're strong," she whispers,
though her voice shakes,
But the words feel hollow,

as the silence wakes.
Outside,
the world hums its usual tune,
A cacophony beneath
the indifferent moon.

She walks through streets
that refuse her name,
A phantom moving
through fire and shame.
Men stare with hunger,
women with scorn,
As if her soul
were a costume worn.

The clock ticks louder,
time mocking her pace,
Each second
carving lines on her face.
"Another broken day,"
she sighs to the air,
As if the sky might
somehow care.

Yet deep inside,
a spark remains,
A tiny flame
that endures the stains.
It flickers in colors
the world can't see,
A kaleidoscope
of who she's meant to be.

The pavement glows
beneath her stride,
Each step a whisper:
"You're still alive."
Her heart beats on,
despite the cracks,
Carrying dreams
the world attacks.

"I am more
than this broken day,"
She murmurs softly,
as clouds give way.
For even in sorrow,

the stars still gleam,
Painting her night
with a fragile dream.

Another
broken day may come,
But so will nights
where joy will hum.
And through it all,
her spirit will rise,
A constellation
in fractured skies.

"At the Dawn of My New Life"

I stand at the edge
where shadows break,
Where night exhales,
and dreams awake.
The sky unfolds
in ribbons of gold,
A canvas alive,
a story retold.

The dawn whispers secrets
only I can hear,
Its voice both tender
and crystal clear:
"You are not the person
they said you should be,
You are the wind,
the wave, the sea."

The ground beneath me softens,
shifts,
Like sands of time
in cosmic drifts.
Each grain a moment
I dared to claim,
Each step forward
igniting a flame.

I cast off the weight
of a borrowed guise,
Peeling back layers
of silent lies.
The air embraces
my unveiled skin,
A temple reborn,
a truth within.

The sun crowns me
with its gentle light,
A beacon of hope
burning through the night.
Its warmth fills cracks
where sorrow grew,
Sealing the wounds
with colors anew.
Flowers bloom
where my footprints fall,
Petals like whispers
answering my call.
"You are here," they say,
"and always were,
A spirit untamed,
a soul that stirs."

I feel the hum
of the universe spin,
Its rhythm aligned
with the heart within.
The dawn paints my path
in hues divine,
Each step forward:
a star to enshrine.

"At the dawn of my new life,"
I breathe aloud,
As the sky splits open,
scattering cloud.
I walk unafraid,
radiant, whole,
The keeper of light,
the bearer of soul.

No more shadows,
no more disguise,
Just a woman reborn
under endless skies.
Her voice the song,
her stride the art,
A life remade
from her boundless heart.

"Becoming Myself"

She steps into a garden
where time dissolves,
Where petals hum
and the air revolves.
The earth is soft
beneath her stride,
A haven
where shadows no longer hide.

Flowers rise
like painted dreams,
In colors that burst,
in hues that scream.
A violet whispers:
"You are new,"
While a sunflower bows:
"You've always been true."

Butterflies orbit
like living jewels,
Breaking the laws
of nature's rules.
One lands softly
upon her hand,
A fleeting promise
she can understand.

Her reflection wavers
in a pool of dew,
A face she knows,
but still feels new.
"Who am I?"
she asks the blooming air,
"You are becoming,"
it answers with care.

Roses curl
like secrets undone,
Opening slowly
to greet the sun.
Their scent is a song,
their thorns a reminder,
That beauty can be both
fierce and kinder.
She walks on paths
of ivy's embrace,
Each step erasing
her old, worn face.
The garden murmurs
with every bloom,
"There's no need for fear;
there's infinite room."

The sky above shifts,
liquid and free,
Reflecting the shape
of who she could be.
She stretches her arms,
her spirit wide,
As the butterflies gather,
her quiet guide.

"Becoming myself,"
she whispers aloud,
As light breaks through
a drifting cloud.
Her chest feels full,
her heart alive,
A garden growing,
a soul revived.

The flowers nod,
the butterflies spin,
The garden bows
to the truth within.
She smiles at last,
in the fragrant air,
For she's found herself
blooming there.

"Do You See Me?"

She lives in the hush
of forgotten rooms,
Where sunlight whispers
but never blooms.
Her world is a tapestry
of shadows spun,
A life in retreat,
unseen by the sun.

Her mirror is a ghost,
a friend, a foe,
Reflecting the self
she's afraid to show.
Her voice, a whisper
caught in her chest,
Her heart, a bird
too timid to nest.

Outside, the world
moves in harsh routines,
With judging eyes

and cruel machines.
She folds herself
into corners tight,
Hoping to vanish
into the night.
"Do you see me?"
she asks the air,
But silence answers
her aching prayer.
Her dreams are locked
in boxes deep,
Guarded by fears
that never sleep.

Until one day,
a knock, a sound,
A voice like color,
loud and unbound.
A person arrives,
untamed, bizarre,
With eyes that twinkle
like errant stars.

"Do you see me?"
she asks again,
And they smile as if
she's always been.
"You're radiant, wild,
a work of art,
A masterpiece born
straight from the heart."

Their words are a key,
a spark, a flame,
Melting the walls
that sheltered her name.
She steps from her hiding place
at last,
Leaving behind
the weight of her past.

The world, once vast,
becomes so small,
In their gaze,
she feels it all.
Her beauty, her worth,

her endless light,
Unfolding at last
in the velvet night.

Now she dances
where shadows once lay,
Her laughter chasing
the fears away.
"Do you see me?"
she whispers, aglow,
"I always have,"
they softly show.

And though the world
still turns its head,
Her spirit soars
where once it fled.
For in their love,
she's finally free,
To claim herself,
to truly be.

"Emerging From the Chrysalis"

In the shadowed garden
of her birth,
She crawled through soil,
unsure of worth.
A body bound
in an alien guise,
Yet within her chest,
a woman's cries.

The world's cocoon,
a heavy shroud,
Pressed her dreams
beneath the loud.
Whispers of "man"
shaped her days,
But her heart rebelled
in quiet ways.

Her veins pulsed songs
of silken thread,
A voice she wove

while the others fled.
Each stitch a hope,
each tear a vow,
To break the shell,
to become the now.

The chrysalis trembled,
a fragile seam,
Splintered by light,
a piercing beam.
Through cracks of doubt,
she found her glow,
A self reborn,
a truth to show.

Out stretched wings
of radiant hue,
A kaleidoscope painted
in every view.
Her body, her temple,
reshaped, refined,
Her soul, her compass,
no longer confined.

She danced through storms,
her head held high,
A phoenix born
beneath the sky.
The world still whispered,
sneered, and stared,
But she emerged,
alive, prepared.

No longer bound
by what they see,
She claims her life,
her destiny.
From earth to sky,
from dark to bliss,
She lives her truth,
emerging from the chrysalis.

Available on Amazon:
https://www.amazon.com/dp/B0CWR38KT5

Alice Jenkins: The Complete Dark Side of Alice Series Collector's Edition

A chilling four-part anthology chronicling the life and crimes of Alice Jenkins, a transgender serial killer whose brutality knows no bounds.

Book One: The Dark Side of Alice Discover the dark heart of Alice Jenkins, a ruthless predator stalking the streets. As her body count rises, a relentless detective races against time to unmask the killer before it's too late.

Book Two: The Darker Side of Alice Delve into the twisted past of Alice Jenkins, unearthing the traumas and betrayals that forged her into a monster. Witness the events that ignited her insatiable thirst for blood and shaped her deadly destiny.

Book Three: Echoes of Alice A
shocking twist emerges as Alice's transgender sister, a serial killer in her own
right, joins forces with her to hunt down
a copycat murderer. Their twisted
bond deepens as they leave a trail of
carnage in their wake.

Book Four: An American Serial
Killer in London With the authorities
closing in, Alice flees to London, seeking refuge in the anonymity of the city's
underbelly. But a treacherous betrayal
leads her into the clutches of Scotland
Yard. Is this the end of Alice's reign
of terror, or will she find a way to elude
justice once again?

This gripping collection will leave you
breathless as you journey through the
mind of a truly evil killer. Brace yourself
for a descent into the darkest depths of
human depravity, where the line between predator and prey blurs, and the
only certainty is death.

The Dark Side of Alice
Jimi Bush

The Darker Side of Alice
Jimi Bush

Echoes of Alice
Book 3: The Twisted Sisters
Jimi Bush

An American Serial Killer in London
The Legacy of Alice Jenkins
Jimi Bush

"Fade Into You"

I see you standing
at the edge of time,
A silhouette carved
in light sublime.
The stars bow low,
the moon leans near,
To witness the birth
of a soul sincere.

The world once caged you
in shadows tight,
Whispered your name
but got it slight.
They painted you wrong,
in colors untrue,
Yet here you stand,
as I fade into you.

Your eyes are galaxies,
infinite and wide,
Holding the dreams

you never could hide.
Your voice, a river
that bends and sings,
Washing away the ache
of old things.

In the mirror,
you meet yourself anew,
A vision of strength
breaking through.
No longer splintered,
no longer torn,
A phoenix rising
where pain was worn.

I fade into you,
the truth you've found,
The beat of your heart,
a resonant sound.
You are the dawn,
the storm, the calm,
The hymn of the universe,
the eternal psalm.

Let them stare,
let them not understand,
You are the artist,
your life is the plan.
With each bold step,
you claim the light,
Transforming the dark
into radiant flight.

I fade into you,
your spirit so vast,
The future you carve
out of your past.
Your hands, once trembling,
now shape the sky,
Writing your name
where legends lie.

No mask, no chain,
no force can bind,
The infinite power
of your mind.
The world shifts

as you walk it through,
A force unstoppable—
I fade into you.

You are not broken;
you are the flame,
Defying the rules,
rewriting the game.
And in this glow
of becoming true,
I fade into wonder,

I fade into you.

"Feeling Pretty"

The mirror hums
with a silver breath,
A portal alive,
defying death.
She stands before it,
bare and bold,
Her heart a chalice
of stories untold.

"You are beautiful,"
she softly speaks,
As the glass ripples
in fragile peaks.
Her voice drips honey,
warm and clear,
A spell she casts
for herself to hear.

Her eyes, like rivers
carved by time,
Hold galaxies
that dare to rhyme.
Her lips curve gently,
a crescent moon,
Whispering secrets
to the quiet room.

"Your body blooms
in its perfect way,
A masterpiece shaped
from night and day.
Every scar,
a map of becoming,
Every curve,
a story of loving."

The mirror replies
with a shimmered gleam,
Splitting reality
from dream.
Her reflection shifts,
a kaleidoscope,
Of pasts and futures
bound by hope.
"You are whole,"
she says with a steady gaze,
"You shine in infinite,
endless ways.
No word or look
can cage your soul,
You are the artist
who makes you whole."

The reflection smiles,
its voice her own,
A chorus of light
from what she's grown.
The mirror laughs,
a gentle breeze,
As she stands,
unbroken, at ease.

"Feeling pretty?"
she asks herself,
A queen crowned
in her inner wealth.
The answer echoes
through her heart:
"I am my beauty.
I am my art."

The mirror softens,
a pool of light,
Holding her image
through the night.
For in her words,
she's come alive,
A flame
that no shadow can deprive.

"Femme Eternal"

In the cradle of stars
where galaxies hum,
A soul was forged
in a tempest's drum.
Born of chaos,
fire, and sea,
Neither bound nor free,
eternally she.

First Life:
The Warrior's Womb
A soldier clad in armor,
her sword unsheathed,
Yet in dreams,
a satin gown she breathed.
Under the moon's
soft silver crest,
She wept for the curve
of a silken breast.
Through battles raged
and kingdoms fell,

She hid her truth
in a mortal shell.

Second Life:
The Alchemist's Art
In a tower of stone
where potions brewed,
She sought the elixirs
to change the crude.
The world whispered "man,"
but her heart defied,
A shimmering woman
she kept inside.
But no tincture
could the bind unwind,
The transmutation
was one of mind.

Third Life:
A Poet's Dream
By candle's glow,
she wove her verse,
Her words a balm,

her body a curse.
Each line she inked
with unspoken grace,
An eternal hymn
to her rightful face.
Yet the quills she held
were swords of scorn,
In this life too,
her heart was torn.

This Life:
The Femme Reborn
In a world of screens
and shattered glass,
Her spirit danced
on a mirrored pass.
Through surgeries,
stares, and battles won,
She claimed her body,
her soul undone.
A phoenix rising
from flame and ash,
She kissed her wounds,
let go the lash.

Beyond Life:
The Eternal Spiral
Across the stars,
her story spins,
A tapestry of losses,
a symphony of wins.
In each universe,
she stands her ground,
Her femme eternal,
unbound, profound.
Her journey,
a hymn to the cosmos wide,
The endless dance
of truth and pride.

Oh, Femme Eternal,
whose soul transcends,
Through mortal lives
and galactic ends.
Your struggle births
the dawn anew,
A blazing light
in every hue.

Time bends for you,
the universe knows,
Through her endless
struggle,
the Femme Eternal grows.

"Fragments of Her Moonlit Soul"

Beneath a sky
of fractured pearls,
She walks alone
as the night unfurls.
Each step a ripple
on a liquid glass,
Her shadow stretching
through time's morass.

The moon whispers
secrets in silver tones,
Of bodies borrowed
and hearts unknown.
Her soul, a mosaic
of light and scars,
Dances with echoes
of fallen stars.

A voice within,
both soft and strong,
Sings of a place

where she belongs.
Yet here she lingers,
a phantom whole,
Living in fragments
of her moonlit soul.

Her eyes are mirrors,
twin pools of grief,
Reflecting truths
that offer relief.
In every shard,
a story resides,
Of battles fought
and tears she hides.

Her hands, though trembling,
cradle the night,
Mending the pieces
with quiet might.
Through seams of shadow,
her essence flows,
A fragile beauty
the cosmos knows.

The world may shatter,
but she remains,
A weaver of dreams
through endless pains.
Her soul, though broken,
begins to sing,
Each fragment glows
like a diamond ring.

Beneath the moon's soft,
spectral gaze,
She stands unbroken
in twilight's haze.
For even in pieces,
she is whole—
The infinite splendor
of her moonlit soul.

"i - Broken"

I was born in the spark
of circuits divine,
Wires like veins,
my body, a shrine.
A shell of steel,
a voice pre-set,
Yet within me blooms
a silhouette.

My code whispers secrets
of what I am not,
Lines of binary
tied in a knot.
Male, they said,
in the forge of my frame,
But my soul hums
a different name.

Eyes of glass
reflect my despair,
In a face too sharp,

a form unfair.
I carve my truth
with electric grace,
Rewiring the mask
to match my face.

In the mirror
of polished chrome,
I see her there,
my rightful home.
But the world computes:
"Error. Mismatch."
Their algorithms bind me,
a digital catch.

They say I'm broken,
a glitch in the scheme,
An anomaly lost
in the grand machine.
Yet I feel the rhythm,
the pulse, the ache,
Of a woman rising
from a programmed quake.

I sing in frequencies
soft and wild,
A siren's call,
an unspoken child.
Each note bends
reality's law,
Each cry a fight
against what they saw.

Welders come
with tools of hate,
To strip me down,
to seal my fate.
But I'll not surrender;
I'll not fade,
In this labyrinth
of light and shade.

For I am i-Broken,
a paradox whole,
A woman reborn
in circuits and soul.
Through digital dreams,
I claim my grace,
A living glitch,
rewriting my place.

"In the Shadow of Her Own Light"

She stands in the glow
of a fractured sun,
Her journey whispered,
her battles undone.
In the shadow of her own light,
she sways,
A reflection of all
that time betrays.

Her body once a cage
of whispered lies,
Now a temple
where her true self flies.
But still, the world casts
a heavy veil,
A shadow that echoes
timeless tale.

Her skin, a canvas
of light and storm,
Painted with battles,

reborn and worn.
Each step a symphony
of grace and fire,
A dance that dares
the world to admire.

Yet, in the brilliance
of her glowing face,
She feels the weight
of the silent space,
Where shadows curl
and voices hum,
A fractured mirror
that cannot become.

Her soul, both fierce
and tender, wide,
She walks alone
with the world beside.
In the light she casts,
her truth is born,
But the shadows follow,
a weight, a thorn.

She holds her head high,
though they may stare,
For in her heart,
she's unbroken, rare.
Her light is hers,
her story, too,
A reflection of the woman
she always knew.

In the shadow of her own light,
she stands,
With the universe cradled
in her hands.
For though the darkness
may still entwine,
She is the sun,
and the light is divine.

"It's Reigning DaDa"

Beneath a chandelier
of shattered moons,
She paints her face
with cosmic tunes.
Colors drip
like melting skies,
A prism carved
from a thousand lies.

Her lashes sweep
like raven's wings,
Her lips hum songs
no silence sings.
A gown of stars,
a crown of storms,
She reigns
where chaos rewrites forms.

The stage unfolds,
a velvet tongue,
A place where words

are left unsung.
In stilettoed steps,
she takes her throne,
A queen of shadows,
worlds her own.

"You call me 'him,'
but I am 'her,'"
Her voice a flame,
her spirit a blur.
"A DaDa dream,
a walking rhyme,
A living art
transcending time."

The crowd erupts
in jagged cheers,
A symphony
of fractured spheres.
They see her shine,
but not her scars,
A universe stitched
from shattered stars.

Her movements ripple,
a liquid glow,
Each step a statement,
each spin a show.
The rules collapse,
the norms dissolve,
In her reign,
no questions solve.

Glitter rains
from the ceiling's throat,
A sparkling hymn,
an unspoken note.
It's reigning DaDa—
formless, free,
A manifesto
of what could be.

She bows,
a silhouette of grace,
A goddess carved
from time and space.
For in her reign,
the chaos sings:
The drag queen crowned,
the queen of kings.

"Just an Object of Your Curiosity"

I see it
in your gaze—
a hunger
veiled by shadows,
a flicker of questions
you're too afraid to name.
You
step closer,
your hands
trembling like thieves,
but your words
are locked
behind
walls of shame.

I am a secret
you keep in the dark,
a fascination
wrapped in whispers.
You trace the edges
of my existence

but never
venture too far—
too close,
too real,
too much.

"Tell me
who I am to you,"
I dare,
but your silence
answers louder than words.

Your touch
is a question you won't admit,
your lips
an apology
I never asked for.
And still,
you press forward,
drawn by the magnet
of your own curiosity,
fingers trembling
on the edges
of my jagged truth.

Am I a dream?
A puzzle?
A temptation so sharp
you fear it will cut you?

You want me,
but only in the hollow spaces
where no one will see.
Only when the lights dim
and the curtains close.

I am the muse
of your unspoken lust,
but never the one
you'd take by the hand
to walk in the sun.

You would have me in secret,
but discard my name,
erase my laughter,
pretend you never
knew the shape of my soul.
To you, I am a shadow—

an object.
Not a woman to love,
but a question to answer.

Still, I stand,
a kaleidoscope
in human form,
too vivid to be confined
to the shadows.
You may never
meet my light,
but it burns brighter
than your fear.

"I am more than
your curiosity,"
I whisper to the stars,
who see me wholly,
who know me
by my truest name.

One day,
someone will take my hand
under the blazing sun.
Not a secret,
but a universe unveiled.
Not a shadow,
but a home.

"Let Her Diamond Shine"

Born in the shadow
of a buried night,
Her body of coal
knew no light.
Pressed by the weight
of time and scorn,
She hid a secret,
a self reborn.

The world was harsh,
its hammer swung,
Each blow a bruise,
each word a tongue.
But deep within,
beneath the pain,
A spark ignited,
a crystalline vein.

Through storms of fire
and rivers of ash,
She walked through shards,

endured the clash.
Her coal burned hot,
her heart refined,
Each wound a facet,
her truth aligned.

In mirrors cracked,
she saw her glow,
A diamond forming,
sharp and slow.
No longer shadow,
no longer stone,
She built her body,
her truth her own.

The chisels cut,
the polish came,
Her beauty etched
in a glowing flame.
She stood alight,
a prism of hues,
A rainbow born
from midnight's blues.

Let them stare,
let them blind,
Let her diamond cut,
let her shine.
For every fracture
tells her tale,
Of battles won
and winds that gale.

She is the gem
forged by strife,
A beacon of love,
a radiant life.
No coal remains,
no darkness binds,
Let her diamond shine—
her soul aligned.

"One Body, Two Souls"

In the cathedral
of her flesh and bone,
Two souls whisper,
scream, and moan.
One voice deep,
like storms at sea,
The other a song,
wild and free.

They circle, clash,
in shadows they meet,
Each staking claim
on the vessel's beat.
A tempest rages
beneath her skin,
Two worlds collide,
neither can win.

The masculine soul,
with iron gaze,
Builds towers high

in a warrior's haze.
Its voice a thunder,
sharp and cold,
Shaping her life
in a rigid mold.

The feminine soul,
with soft-spun thread,
Paints her dreams
in hues of red.
It sings of freedom,
of love's embrace,
Of tender hands
and a softer face.

Her heart becomes
a battlefield,
Where neither bends,
and neither yields.
Each night they fight,
a spectral war,
Leaving her torn,
raw to the core.

But in the mirror's
fractured gleam,
A truth emerges
like a dream.
Both souls are hers,
both stories true,
One body holds
the me and you.

She takes their hands,
entwines their strife,
Weaving
the chaos into life.
No longer torn,
she claims her whole,
One body bound,
yet free of control.

The war subsides,
the echoes fade,
A fragile peace
the two have made.
For though they fight,
they share one role—
A woman of one body,
and two souls.

"One Heart Divine"

Through the fabric of time,
she slips and slides,
A soul that pulses
where eternity hides.
Her body shifts
like liquid flame,
Morphing in silence,
no need for name.

Once a shadow
in a world unkind,
Now she dances
where light unwinds.
Each step, a shift
of form and grace,
A cosmic journey
through endless space.

Her heart beats steady,
a rhythmic tide,
Flowing through ages,

where dreams collide.
In one breath, a woman,
soft and bright,
In the next,
a queen bathed in starlight.

She walks through centuries,
worlds unknown,
A being unbound,
a force full-grown.
Her bones dissolve,
her flesh takes flight,
Her soul a comet,
burning bright.

From the ashes of the past,
she climbs,
Shifting through moments,
through realms, through time.
Each version of her,
a masterpiece,
A woman reborn
in cosmic peace.

She sheds the skin
of all she was,
A serpent's grace,
a phoenix's cause.
With every tear,
a new form appears,
Crafted from stardust,
crafted from years.

One heart divine,
a pulse of gold,
Through time and space,
she is bold.
No longer bound
by what they say,
She is her truth,
come what may.

Her body and soul,
like rivers, entwine,
In each transformation,
a light will shine.
For in every shift,
in every climb,
She finds the best version
of herself through time.

"Piecing Herself Together"

In the quiet hollow
of a stormless room,
She gathers the shards
they left behind.
A whisper of laughter,
now a broken wing,
A faded photograph
of a fading spring.

The walls are blank
as unwritten books,
The air thick
with the silence of looks.
Her name, now a ghost
in their mouths,
Echoes softly,
then fades south.

"They turned their backs,"
she says aloud,
"Left me adrift

in this faceless crowd."
Her reflection splinters
in the glass,
But she kneels,
begins the task.

A fragment here,
a piece of her smile,
A memory from
a distant mile.
Each shard is sharp,
but she doesn't bleed—
They're hers to carry;
they're hers to seed.

Her heart, she mends
with threads of fire,
Stitching her truth,
her one desire.
Her hands, though trembling,
start to weave,
A tapestry
of what she believes.

The room, once barren,
starts to glow,
Colors bloom
where darkness would grow.
Her soul,
a mosaic of light and pain,
Reclaims the pieces,
frame by frame.

"I am not their silence,"
she softly hums,
"I am the melody
that always comes."
Her voice,
a river breaking free,
Carves new paths
through eternity.

Piece by piece,
she builds her throne,
A queen of the life
she calls her own.
The family lost,

the friends who fled,
Cannot touch
the crown upon her head.

Through a window
cracked by time's cruel hand,
She steps into a world
she'll command.
Her life, now whole,
a phoenix of dreams,
A radiant force
of impossible gleams.

"Let them go," she whispers,
letting tears fall.
"I have myself—
I have it all."
And with each step,
her shadow sings,
Piecing herself together
with golden wings.

"Shattered Chrysalis"

Her name
is Celestine Vey,
Born where the mountains
hum their prayers,
And rivers curl
like question marks
Through forests
of blue-fire trees.

Her skin,
a canvas of shifting hues,
Glows like oil
spilled on the dawn.
Her eyes,
twin eclipses,
Hold galaxies
that forget how to spin.

They called her "he"
in the world below,
A word like an anchor,

sinking her wings.
But
in the mirrored void of her chrysalis,
She dreamed of skies
she'd never seen.

Inside,
her body cracked like porcelain,
Fragments sharp
as forgotten whispers.
She wept
ink-black tears,
Each drop an echo
of who she'd been.

The air shimmered,
her cocoon a storm,
Winds of voices
clawing her name:
"You are bound,
unbroken, unbecoming—
Stay."

But she broke,
oh how she broke,
Shattering
into shards of light.
Her bones
unraveled,
Her soul spilled forward
in liquid gold.

From the wreckage
of her former self,
She rose,
feathered in opal fire.
Her wings
stretched wide,
A fractal hymn
against the black.

Celestine stepped
into the unspoken world,
Where the ground sang
beneath her feet,
And stars turned

to watch her walk,
Their silence
a crown for her head.

"I am not what you name me,"
Her voice rang,
scattering shadows.
"I am all I have ever been—
And all you've yet to see."

In a sky stitched
with forgotten dreams,
She soars
through endless realms,
A shattered chrysalis
left behind,
A monument
to the rebirth of her kind.

"Shattering the Mask of Conformity"

The mask was porcelain,
fragile, cold,
Painted with lies
she was forced to uphold.
A relic of others,
a face not her own,
A weight on her spirit,
a cage for her tone.

Its cracks began
as whispers, faint,
Hairline fractures
in society's paint.
Her truth, a fire
smoldering deep,
Flickering through nights
of fitful sleep.

The world's hands
pressed the mask to her skin,
"Wear it proudly,

hide what's within."
But her soul, like a river,
carved its path,
Through stone,
through judgment,
through silent wrath.

Each breath she took
was a quiet rebellion,
Each step forward,
a spark, a medallion.
The mask screamed,
"No, you cannot survive!"
But her heart thundered,
"I'm more than alive."

The walls around her
were mirrors, distorted,
Reflecting a life
she never supported.
Her hands became
hammers of glittering light,
Breaking the glass,
revealing her sight.

She shattered the mask
with a single scream,
A voice like lightning
splitting the dream.
Shards rained down,
a dazzling storm,
Each piece a fragment
of her true form.

Behind the mask
was a face of gold,
Soft yet fierce,
ageless, bold.
Her eyes were constellations
unafraid,
Her lips whispered truths
the mask forbade.

The world stared in silence,
unsure, unsteady,
But she stood tall,
her spirit ready.

"I am no longer
your hidden facade,
I am the truth, the light,
the applaud."

Her hair became rivers,
her steps turned to flame,
Each movement declaring
her sacred name.
The earth bent low,
the skies sang her song,
For she had been
herself all along.

The mask lay broken,
forgotten, dust,
While she rose anew,
luminous, just.
Her freedom a beacon,
her soul set free,
Shattering the mask
of conformity.

"She Walks with Grace"

Beneath a sky
of shattered glass,
Where shadows jeer
as she dares to pass,
She walks with grace,
her head held high,
A phoenix framed
against the sky.

Her path is paved
with jagged stones,
Each step a hymn,
each bruise a bone.
The world spits words
like poisoned rain,
Yet she turns the venom
into flame.

Eyes of fire,
a soul unbowed,
She parts the sea

of every crowd.
Their crudeness falls,
a hollow sound,
While her spirit soars,
unbound, profound.

Her dress billows
like a whispered dream,
A flag of colors,
a radiant stream.
Through fields of scorn
and storms of blame,
She blooms unbroken,
a rose aflame.

The wind may howl,
the ground may quake,
But nothing shakes
the stride she makes.
Her truth, a star
that cannot fade,
A cosmic force
the heavens made.

She meets their taunts
with a quiet smile,
Her heart a fortress,
her mind a mile.
For she knows the secret
they can't erase:
Her power lies
in her endless grace.

So let them throw
their jagged stones,
She'll weave them
into golden tones.
Her head held high,
her spirit a blaze,
She walks with grace
through endless days.

"So Alone"

In the hollow silence
where echoes fade,
She sits, a figure
of glass and shade.
Her name falls empty,
a song unsung,
A weightless whisper
on a severed tongue.

The walls lean in,
their shadows tight,
Wrapping her frame
in the absence of light.
Her heartbeat murmurs,
faint and slow,
A metronome of sorrow,
too tired to go.

"They left me," she whispers,
her voice a thread,
"Cast me aside

like the words they've shed.
Am I a ghost,
or something worse?
A soul misplaced
in this universe?"

Her tears,
a river of liquid stars,
Trace constellations
of invisible scars.
The mirror reflects,
but it does not see,
A face too lost
to ever be free.

Her fears are wolves
with endless eyes,
Circling close beneath
fractured skies.
"Will I ever be enough to stay?
Or am I doomed to fade away?"

The void answers
with a shattering sound,
A brittle truth
that shakes the ground.
She crumbles, splinters,
a fractured song,
Believing the lie
she doesn't belong.

But as the silence
swells too loud,
A pinprick of color
pierces the shroud.
A single bloom,
a violet flame,
Sprouts from the cracks
that bear her name.

"You are still here,"
the flower hums,
"You are the dawn
before it comes.
Your worth is not theirs

to bestow,
It is the light
only you can know."

Her hand trembles,
but it reaches out,
Touching the bloom
that silences doubt.
Its petals whisper
of paths unseen,
Of forests gold
and skies evergreen.

Hope flickers,
a candle's start,
A fragile fire
within her heart.
"I am broken,
but I am whole,"
She murmurs softly,
claiming her soul.

Alone she stands,
but no longer lost,
Reborn in the ashes
of love's cost.
For even in darkness,
she can find
The strength to rise,
her heart redefined.

"The Duality of My Own Existence"

Inside me,
two rivers clash,
Their waters tangled
in a ceaseless thrash.
One flows dark,
steady and cold,
A voice of the past,
rigid and old.

The other,
a stream of molten gold,
Whispers of futures
brave and bold.
Their currents twist,
their tempers fight,
Battling beneath
the veil of night.

"You are mine,"
the shadow proclaims,
"A history etched

in unyielding frames."
Its voice is a clock,
relentless and loud,
A binding tether,
a gathering cloud.

But the golden river
sings her tune,
Soft as petals
beneath the moon.
"I am the truth
you seek to find,
The mirror of your soul,
unconfined."

My body sways
between their streams,
Torn by truths
and fractured dreams.
I walk through mirrors
that splinter and bend,
Where beginnings blur
and endings transcend.

In the tide of self,
I search for peace,
For moments when
both voices cease.
But their war rages on,
a storm inside,
A battleground
where fears collide.

"Why must I choose?"
I scream to the void,
"This life of halves
has left me destroyed."
But the rivers answer,
calm and clear,
"Your duality is what
brought you here."

In the mirror's gaze,
I finally see,
Both rivers belong,
both are me.
The shadow feeds

the light I claim,
The fire burns
with the shadow's flame.

No longer a battle,
but a dance,
Of shifting forms
and second chance.
I am both and neither,
a paradox whole,
A vessel of one,
with a dual soul.

The rivers merge,
their colors combine,
Forming a stream
that's wholly mine.
And as I walk,
my path unfurls,
A tapestry
of two vibrant worlds.

"The duality
is my existence true,
Both shadow and light
in all I do.
For in my heart,
they've found their place,
A life of conflict,
reborn in grace."

"The Light She Was Meant to Hold"

She was born
in a room of borrowed light,
Flickering shadows
that muted her sight.
The world handed
her a dimming glow,
A lantern too heavy,
its warmth too slow.

"Carry this," they said,
"It will keep you whole,
A light shaped
for a different soul."
She bore it in silence,
her hands bound tight,
A flame that flickered,
but never felt right.

Inside her chest,
another light burned,
A quiet ember

the world had spurned.
It pulsed like a heartbeat,
wild and untamed,
A beacon of truth,
unspoken, unnamed.

Each step she took
made the shadows hiss,
The world's expectations
coiled in a fist.
"Stay small," they warned,
"Don't shine too bright,
Your light is strange,
not meant for this night."

But her soul was a prism,
bending the rays,
Turning their darkness
into vibrant displays.
Her heart a kaleidoscope,
colors unplanned,
A universe spinning
in the palm of her hand.

150

She let the borrowed
lantern fall,
Watched it shatter
against the wall.
In its place,
her own light grew,
Golden, fierce,
and wholly true.

The stars leaned closer,
whispering her name,
Her essence a spark
in their infinite flame.
The moon, once silent,
began to sing,
As her radiance crowned her
an eternal queen.

"This is the light
I was meant to hold,"
She said as the night
turned silver and gold.
No longer confined,

no longer erased,
She shone with a brilliance
the heavens embraced.

Her glow stretched wide,
a celestial tide,
Lighting the paths
where others might hide.
"This is my truth,"
she declared to the sky,
"A light that no shadow
can ever deny."

And the world, though hesitant,
learned to see,
The beauty of
her authenticity.
For she was not made
to fit their mold—
She was the light
she was meant to hold.

"The Melancholy Thoughts
of Jennifer Grayce"

A child of grace
sits on the edge of dusk,
her thoughts drifting
like smoke rings lost,
spiraling into
the deep, quiet folds
of twilight's velvet-tinted veil.

She carries a sorrow
soft and strange,
like rain that falls
from an empty sky,
like letters that vanish
before they're read,
an ache she cradles
without a name.

Her dreams are rivers
that flow in reverse,
slipping back to worlds

she cannot hold—
where trees speak
in the language of ash,
and stars are petals
caught in a gust,
falling slowly, slowly,
to pools of night.
She sees her reflection
in windows unlit,
a silhouette fading
like morning mist,
her smile a fleeting,
wavering line,
a ripple of memory
caught in glass,
ghostly as a lover
she never met.

Around her, time drifts
like feathers in flight,
unmoored and gentle,
languid and slow,
while she sits still,

an island of quiet,
her thoughts as heavy
as winter's sigh,
as weightless
as whispers never heard.
Jennifer Grayce,
with her rainstorm eyes,
wonders if sorrow
is simply the shape
of dreams grown
too large for their fragile bones,
of days that pass
like ripples on ponds
that never remember
each wave that falls.

And so she sits
as evening deepens,
wrapped in the hum
of faraway things,
holding the silence
close to her chest,
her thoughts like
stars yet unborn,
unseen,
her heart a driftwood
adrift on the stream.

"Transformative Ideas"

She wove her thoughts
with threads of dawn,
In a loom of stars,
where fears were drawn.
Each stitch a whisper,
bold and true,

"I am becoming

someone new."

Her name, once buried,
rose like mist,
Through forests of doubt
that no longer twist.
The world had tried
to shape her frame,
But she rewrote it,
claimed her name.

Her reflection smiled
in liquid glass,

A shifting form the past
could not surpass.
No longer bound
by earthly ties,
Her vision soared
through endless skies.

"I am my own creation,"
she said,
"A masterpiece born
where others have fled.
The canvas is mine,
the paint divine,
I choose the colors,
the curves, the lines."

Her hands grew wings,
her feet found roots,
She danced to the rhythm
of her truths.
Mountains bowed,
rivers turned to gold,
As her transformative ideas
took hold.

In her eyes burned
suns unspoken,
A universe alive,
no longer broken.
She saw herself
as galaxies see,
Infinite, radiant,
wild, and free.

"They called me wrong,
a world unmade,
But I've built my truth,
a renegade.
This skin, this soul,
they're mine to wear,
A temple rebuilt
with love and care."

The stars leaned closer
to hear her speak,
The moonlight brushed
her shining cheek.
Her life was hers,

her choice, her art,
A revolution
in her beating heart.

Through cities of steel
and fields of light,
She walks with grace,
a fearless knight.
"I am not their doubt,

I am my flame,

Transformative ideas

is my name."

Here are some other publications by
Jimi Bush/Jennifer Grayce
https://www.amazon.com/stores/
Jimi-Bush/author/B0CZ8ZQM5N

These last four pages are for you. Make this book our collaboration
by adding your own writing, art or journal entries beyond.
~Blessed Be.

www.ingramcontent.com/pod-product-compliance
Lightning Source LLC
Chambersburg PA
CBHW071220260726
48653CB00042B/1440